NOT ALL HONEY

RODDY LUMSDEN

NOT ALL HONEY

BLOODAXE BOOKS

ISBN: 978 1 78037 112 2

First published 2014 by
Bloodaxe Books Ltd,
Eastburn,
South Park,
Hexham,
Northumberland NE46 1BS.

www.bloodaxebooks.com
For further information about Bloodaxe titles
please visit our website or write to
the above address for a catalogue.

Supported using public funding by
**ARTS COUNCIL
ENGLAND**

Cover design: Neil Astley & Pamela Robertson-Pearce.

Printed in Great Britain by Bell & Bain Limited, Glasgow, Scotland, on
acid-free paper sourced from mills with FSC chain of custody certification.

for Isabelle Boyer,
The Princess of Burma, always

ACKNOWLEDGEMENTS

Acknowledgements are due to the following publications and websites where some of the poems were published: *The Great British Bard Off*, *Edinburgh Review*, *Gutter*, *Magma*, *Oxford Poetry*, *Poems in Which*, *Poetry International*, *Poetry Proper*, *Poetry School*.

Thanks to ABJ as ever for his thoughts and to Amy Key and Heidi Seppälä for loving friendship and support during difficult times.

CONTENTS

Farewell to Bread

The papers said that I was thinner.

In another life, I was a commissionaire
or caricaturing tourists in some difficult city.

I was thinking Venice was a no.

I shouldn't have grumped on Annie, but
I didn't know her dog had died.

As I've said before, no one should cover 'Life on Mars'.

I was trying to figure a way of putting
an epigraph before an epigraph.

I was a cipher in my own petty system of abandon.

I was wondering how long we'd have to wait for
Gill-and-Alex, which seems inevitable.

I was wondering how much of this could make it into Latin.

I thought of Sinéad asleep. Her sneeze.

I had bidden farewell to bread.

By 'the papers' I mean whichever papers.

I recalled what Imo said about size and attraction and felt it
like a gun quite close to my head, by which I mean cold and true.

I was tired of people westering at me,
gimping over their phones.

I regretted promising Greg new winklepickers.

I felt uncomfortable that someone might ask
which of the younger poets I found most attractive.

I was hung and drawn.

When I argued internally, it was generally with you, friend.

I was fond of the Conroys.

I was fond of my own blood, its cameo appearances.

I worried that people called *Geier Gaier* and *Faycal Faisal.*

I tried to remember the last time I had said 'no' to anything.

I thought of when I hugged Charlie and she said,
'but you don't like people touching you.'

It was clear I had allies and that was something.

My sexual fantasy about Sally is the least explicit –
not even a nipple, not even a sigh.

I was toying with my chances of survival under the circumstances.

I was thinking of Kathy – new book – but is she happy?

I wondered how Simon sleeps, all those murdered children
swimming in his eyes.

I uninvented the sandwich. I worked on
the square root of my happiness.

I tried saying no. Like this – NO. But no one was convinced.

HOPE VERSUS DOUBT

Hope

When you looked right at me, I became
the harbour wall, or the grim boards
of the cart which my great grandfather
rolled down from, to his ditch and drown.

I do not snap, but if I snapped I'd rather
it would be this cutty hurt, this town,
a dumb approximation of the same
small sound, a kitty inkling, minor hoard.

I sense things thinning, but keep a word
which skirts all pithy stops, bilks blame
and spills me to that rosy edge of other
where down is out, and out shut down.

Stockholm Syndrome

I stand accused of misdemeanours: an overactive
desire to hold you, captive,

of knowing where the berries are in surfeit,
of being their itching herald,

becoming the hustle's seldom one –
look out Broadway! I'm all surface! –

of knowing the brisking end of the start
of something (*vertraue mir*, sour world)

need not be the beginning of its end.
For see it written here on pretty paper:

the hostage may in time accept the taker.
Have you seen my light, welcomed one,

have we changed? And my especial art
is to capture some *forever* from mere *fond*.

Sometimes you step out for that missing stair
and find it's there.

Self, Rising

There comes a day when you realise
El Greco lived long before the sugar cube.

You are reading about Hilaire Belloc
while listening to 'Don't Fear the Reaper',

You are thinking of knocking up a chowder,
one Beckett might appreciate, although

you know he would prefer the window ajar,
the soft hustle of a village cricket game.

You wish you were better at cakes, the sort
your dexterous flatmate conjures so easily:

chevrons of zippy sponge, chocolate numerals,
soppy thoughts baked to amorous conclusion.

Even the filthiest lie will take air and soar.
There are frogs smaller than a thumbnail,

rabbitlings nimbling in cages on the Ramblas,
some moments are best not spent thinking big.

It's fine not to be sure of dragee and angelica,
to find arrowroot and mace not at the back

of your spice drawer, but in the hinterlands
of fluctuant persuasions – you can't know all.

It's coming on five, it's the tail of summer,
so something must give in the sifting game

of detach, caution, pang. Far cities drift,
islands turn slow on their igneous masts;

though the wheel is invented, the biggest one
is always yet to be hoisted and spun up.

A fallen nickel glints in the skyscraper's shadow;
a gaptooth girl knee-high to a model of Wadlow.

The strangest things we harbour are much like
smudges around the mouth, oafish smooches,

paintbox mishaps, cream smears, all told,
the day's a mystery package, so preheat the oven,

heave out the mixing bowl. Most days you count
the times you have fallen hard. It's not enough.

Kir Royale

I was slow counting slow hours
and thinking the day was wasted,
when the storm came, first

thunder's groan, then a minute count
and thumping rain and, pressed
to the balcony door, I thought again

of the bubbles in those cocktails
with which we started, that night
we got wasted in Barcelona

and how earlier I had watched,
patient and proud with foretaste,
as you were readying to venture out,

your graceful bob, your mirrored face,
where pink was added to the pale,
much as the cassis sweetens its glass,

just as it's the blast and bob of fizz
which charms the eye, and yet
it's something truer which intoxicates.

Firebirds

*The crisis consists precisely in the fact that the old
is dying and the new cannot be born*

ANTONIO GRAMSCI

So the rare-eyed chick, unhatched,
cannot be true bird yet
not till its fadding dame sees through
her half millennium
and scuffs up into flames.

The little swimmer too
is not quite human, the ink still wet,
the glue not fixed, its albion
a hike away, one eye to the latch
of day, through which it sucks its tricks.

For in the bout of fire, two
become none: the slow match
of hope versus doubt on which you bet
too much. From robe of shell or amnion
the frothy head coils out.

Women in Paintings

The masters laboured – *all the hours of the clock* –
to clone the ringlets of a marchioness or pull
a cape of dark around the head of an ecstatic saint.

Portraiteers talked low and long to captive sitters,
so Boleyn's swan neck can still be kissed, Jill
last in a steel blue frock, before my parents met.

And in *Sous Bois*, Corot threw down a lilac twister
of a sunstreak, through which the bonneted girl
is ever about to step, daydreaming of candied fruit.

Day yields to dusk. The artful lie takes awful work.
We strive words from the loath core of our will:
You will be loved again. Everything'll be all right.

Calumet

I was working up a list of the great winter cities
and sipping soda water from a crystal glass
when from the next room I heard a radio, or rather
two radios, tuned to separate channels, or perhaps
one radio and one recording of that same radio,
or another radio, say, or two recordings of a radio.

Then, setting down my pencil, I could discern,
through the double churn of voices, more subtle
instances: the relieved pop of soap bubbles
in a basin or the sound of a pipe being sparked
then drawn on in a place that pleasure has missed,
but where there is release, load then overload.

Epithalamion

Towards a theory to explain how
nothing remains the same: a person
will burden with age or bird down;
the sea fails to make an impression
on itself, of itself. Night sky hustles
in the mutability of gravity and dust;

the statues in some sun-stung court
sway in this heat; the folly bristles
as its bricks thicken with noon rain;
or what you didn't know would turn:
a sweet lens spilling the spectrum
from a mile long banderole of light.

Yet to unchange also is to change:
a stasis you forge in time from your
sprint of boldened thought or that blur,
the stillicidal blear of a yard tap's drip.
Unchange also is to change sun-up,
tide wooze, willows at a river's fringe.

And doubt could not stalk this view:
its lair found cold, grit of its bones
in the cave's black sand. A proving
would not loot such blithe concord.
For aim. For action. Sure. For you
who, giving, intuit sense of giving

into it. Towards the apple's chance
of finding earth, blood luck of veins
which run with wonder. The melody
made twice thus becoming harmony
in which the choosers give sure word,
for which we watchers save our dance.

To James Brookes at 25

The komakino audience filing in, pale to the neck,
pale from it. Next door, a diehard tanner's goggles
are sound nuts of the blackest plastic and he lies
thinking of the greyest greys in all Mitteleuropa.

The film, undoubtedly, is black and white: suits
zoom in alleys, a clockface does its glimmering,
rooms caught for art's duration bustle in off-tones
which knew the swig of the editor's styro beaker.

Vita brevis. High history? Its fever shanks roam
the pitchy bounds. Cervantes at a mirror combs
his soft, white hair, Pablo fusses grey with grey
to make the proper grey. Answers are questioned.

I'd heard the way was sweetly mown, all green gone
as the hot press chanked off one thousand copies
of some dirty tract. Then a stranger noticed a scuff
of yellow in the pearl, another the quiet pink of it.

Photograph of Emily Hasler Napping

Not on a rope swing. Not in cocktail chic.
Never in a jeep and not macheteing yams.
Not randoming, at least not evidently.
Not at present passing any parcel, not
leading that pirate mutiny, neither minotaur
nor sphinxish. Not nearing Waverley Station,
singing out 'Mama'. And never swimming
the Rhine, in Basel, after a polymer seminar.

Always seeming though, schooled in arrival.
Shoeless, one assumes, and aiming inwardly
to best of destination. Swimming hope's fosse.
Flies scam the window, the commentator irks.
A half-read book, minor to this whole scene,
has taken half a year to topple; now it does.

For Charlotte

Because you are uncunningly beautiful and less
than half my age, I am wary of starting this, should
anyone bring doubt to even one stitch of my intention.
I was you once, still am you, always trying to run
one inch ahead of the garish river of troubledness.
Worst days, I'd lie flat to the floor of my parents' room,
not my own; the light was always colder there and I felt
more *with* my banishment from what never knew me.
It gets better. Then often it gutters back. Doctors
shiver in your sight. You are drawn to the road's middle,
to march it fierce. I do not know what you will be.
Though I sense something, able runner with lava
at your heels. That times will be righted. Or diagonal
at least. An inch is all you need, though you still feel heat.
The ostrich wins by running. The running little foxes
beneath my window do not know their dens are shallow.
Rumoured systems betray us. Light filches some way in.
I see cameras. I see rostrums. Some days, all the tech
dries us. And we are wet things, all that dummy blood.
Run then? Not to tempts us. Quiet, that mentioned thing,
lurks, not close to touch. Quiet at the garden's border,
quiet in a fussless room. Rush, though. Need, hope.
Rush. Maybe some pitchy day you will need to run,
and I'll be elsewhere, others will be darning, caroling,
hanging washing. All this wavers towards the not fair.
Not, not. But allow, allow and, lass, if need be, run.

On First Meeting Margot

When you were born, they said
you looked like me – as if – if only –
but now I see your Daddy's eyes
right away, and think how fond I am
of him, as you twist around
your mother, pranking, having a busy day.
And your mother is still bringing off
the perfection, as she ever has.
Margot, I'm concussed. One day
you'll know what that means. Each minute,
or so, I tell myself, beneath my breath,
'be careful'. Today I counted the people
I truly love and didn't use too many fingers.
I can't play the classical guitar, have never
slalomed and rum does very little for me.
I'm still in love with someone
who is growing uncomfortable with that.
I have limited patience for theatre,
of the real or metaphorical sorts.
Excuse me, Margot, I am introducing myself
somewhat awkward, but you seem
anyhow to prefer spinning round Mummy,
more than my persuasive interference.
Your shy smile is the best of it.
You will talk any dog off a ledge.
You will shuck both Egham and Swindon,
being the new breed. Luck dances
as you dance. All will be all will be best.
I will mend as you grow, important one.
I shake your hand in stately fashion.
Lady, that was a blessing to meet you.
To be that. It was a day of remark.

Shanties of Tinie Hope

Nemarca

It's the sea, you said, *we should be cautious.*
And I thought *crook frightfulness*, thought
all manner. And being both of the river
and the sea, I wondered which direction
we might swim. And your new room
was a shade baronial but bludgeoned
with books and you read to me in bed.

Then I thought of Nemarca's porch,
that ambivalent song space, neither
in or outdoors, and the shamey tang
of your pudding bowl ashtray, the dead
seabird you told me of, and how all life
is a jinx of doubling, and we lay the night
doubled or halved, a to-be-written song.

Naumachia

If I fold my hand and knock the ocean,
I might cobble one for you, or might
ambrosially engineer it, a felucca
laden with fat currants scuppered,
a pirate tub shooken down to the weed,
a winged sea serpent charming off
the heads of ten doomed oarsmen.

Swords, glooms, blackest of parallels
you may not want, but the gesture,
the gasconade: my head stutters yes.
The heart hunts your darling island,
a blue boat, two sized, and wonder
daring my approach and you singing,
Fetch me, sailor, I will travel with you.

Nomicon

Two destinations I am keen to avoid:
death and space. I see myself spatchcocked
on Aldebaran, numbed by sulphurous fury.
So I list the list of the ones I have held
which ends with you. And doubt and hope,
that twiceness, that laced talk of cherries
or dates seething in their ripened tide.

Choose one? I've heard a ship might list,
its tummy full of spices, full of yesterday.
Law or image. Yet we are sea folk, girl,
that tide will run for us and we will run
for it. And if I am gone, still sing this:
The day blue fell and I fell blue
until the sea washed in with you.

Myokymia / Carrie Fisher

Ihana tanssija, when you left, I felt the tundra,
laughter in a nearby room, noir rememberings.
Plates lacked sheen. Your sequins on the carpet
catch still on my twitchy eye. How many times,
I asked, have people thought I am winking at them?
A man followed me home in Edinburgh,
thinking I was wanting him. A few wide eyes.
Daddy / daughter – yes, that's what we were,
but sometimes me the daughter, I'd have to say,
as you shepherdessed me, not knowing my route
across the stepping stones. Twice in my life,
I have nearly met Carrie Fisher. I moved to the sofa,
because she was staying, at my brother's place,
before you were born. She never did arrive.
I have never seen *Star Wars*. Bella loves *Star Wars*.
A decade back, a mutual friend said Carrie and I
were surely likeminded, and that we should meet.
I spilled on that, the famous being not my notion.
First night you moved in, you took your hair down,
your stagey make-up off, appeared in the hallway
of our Prendergast Zoo, in those kitten pyjamas.
I feared I'd fall for you, but it was a different love
we brewed. Careful business. Sorting one another.
Sure, sure I miss you, and the soup I made you
and your supple way, and the giant wedding dress
we stored beneath my bed. I know a little Finnish.
A little. Moi moi. And when you left, you said,
'good luck with your class', but I heard instead
'good luck with your plans'. Ouch, I have no plans.
And I said back, 'Farewell Tanssija', as I climbed
down four flights to the real world. Luck unlocks us,
and steals our stuff. I have long done with luck.

Do you think I should try a third time with Carrie?
I think she would shrug. I fear we might small talk.
Heidi, we became strange muscles in one another.
You slurped tea, went for pirates, risked, risked,
and rose. But I know the rose placed on my grave
will likely be from you. Moi moi. Wink, wink.

The Tao of Amy Key

That there is a world I need to escape to.
I reached 48 and achieved my first box file.
I settle all my handouts in it, serenely.
That there are things which make me glad:

the box file, the Village, bottle green, seeing
Sarah appear in the distance, waving ahoy.
Sarah is Chinese, halfway through. Amy
is yet to achieve the will to be Chinese.

But her aspects seem such, as she has a path.
She has one child, which is her cherished self.
She moves in partial peace over grassland.
Her revolutions are mostly in the past.

Satin is perhaps Chinese and satin is Amy.
The natural and mercurial outcomes of action
mean she is essentially nameless though we think
on both warm and wet days of her as Amy.

I throw sticks and then I crack the I Ching
and the page that opens talks clearly of us,
walking on the Rye, discussing foo yung,
how soft it should be, the beating procedures

which bring super effect. Gunpowder appears
on occasion. That there is paper, coloured,
vintage thises and thats. That our thriving
should not indulge curveball dalliances

with givers of crumbs. Now think of why
a box file could contain most of things,
even a dinosaur, or a dubious lexicon:
the cryptic needs its sorting, its box file.

Cultivation of the way needs melon ballers
and dinky glasses for elderflower cocktails.
The essential energy of action and existence
asks politely for a Dutch door, brisk kittens

and a toothsome starter that takes an hour
to burst into most absolute belief. That
the way to integrity is to move, somewhat,
like a harpsichordist, in contrast to the linear,

invoking a cycle. I look behind me to witness
Kongzi on my balcony – he is leafing *Luxe*
and on his headphones, 'Don't Bring Lulu'
swerves into 'Hobart Paving'. We have all

been there. By which I mean that world to
try to escape. That trinkets might bend a mind.
That there is escape to and also escape from.
That there is doubleness of notioned harmony

and all other harmony. I would further explain
but Kongzi is knocking at the glass. His brow
wrinkles. He has found a line which troubles
and pleases in equilibrium. Can I help him?

Paul Risi

Was that young Paul Risi just finding his feet
or a trick of the light upon Nicholson Street?

GORDON GRAHAME, 'Belfast'

If I knew you, I do not know I knew you
but I hear you died young and which of us
hasn't hankered after pulling off that trick,
only to pull back into the yolk of our sustaining?

And your name is here and there still, your name
breathing in me charms its one black dream
of distinction. We met, and we talked, or not.
I held a door for you. We passed on party stairs.

The rose does this, the ranging coin, the moon
we ought not mention, easy as it is. Damp nags
we're less than. The young dead, pantheoned
in blasted circumstance, those who had to.

Yet I know that's wrong, even in the hive
of the little I do know. Say, Nicholson Street
which I have as I have jowls, a kiss curl,
tears for music, a swoop of past which tricks

to say I knew you, if and that I did. In student flats,
my friends talked of going early, but lay late, steamed,
three to a room, dreamed beyond buttered pasta,
stoned jokes, plectrums, to where our songs

might brave cliffs and towers, grow soft fruit the lost
would taste. I've not enough of you, I'm hamming up
this loss. You were there though. Our eyes met and when
you walked past, you knew me for what I was.

At Whitby Abbey

Precision skims, since grey and green
are fine cogs of the same simmering machine

as friction grims between each aim and sky
intuiting intention's alibi

as vigour wells and withers in accordance
with the licking flame of my affordance

belief in which is no less easy than
the songbird's two note claim: I am.

Fear of Ice Cream

Scarborough 5/1/12

Kam Sang: red ribbons of char siu
topple inside the rice bowl – one
avalanche I will step cleanly into,
asking, who whistled? Who sang?

*

The hare, nearing end, will race
toward the dragon. *Self* and *else*
in perpetual impasse. What goes
without saying: all love sees fear.

*

And Lucas, his unbonny aunt tries
to spoon ice cream into his pursed
Cupid's bow; cold is all but death
upon the lips of the infant startled.

*

Scunnerations: the paltry spieling;
the guilt of swanking it à la carte;
Glaswegians yatting two tables
behind; any song with whistling.

*

The tanked carp have one trick:
the surge and surf as, fishfully,
they broach at the aerator's flux,
are nixed in a snub of bubbles.

*

A thin oil junk sails pell mell over
Kowloon harbour; the sky's queasy,
the sea Quink, the moon a vanilla
trinket from a former rival's poem.

*

A plastic wall hanging of Buddha
is more Slime than jade. To get to
my point: I'm speaking here to you,
lost love, of the sea and of purpose.

*

What then of our private hells?
All cusses in this damned chain
have a chasm into which to spoon
their wintry lacks of substance.

*

Buddha in Peasholm Park, a stone
hand raised, anywhere in a century
of welcoming, braving all frost
in a roost of Michaelmas daisies.

*

A mandarin drake poised, and sure
I do mean poised, on the lastmost
weir. The one most purposefully not
listening is the one you want to hear.

*

Unseasoned. Off season. As luteus
and catkin and sweet tea rose then
the rusting of the swathes step into
the cypher: a pre-Möbius Möbius.

*

North Marine Rd: just not enough
pain to claim nostalgia. Yet Regent
St is followed by Hope St. The view
at last gives in to the new year's sea.

*

But down sidestreets (sigh) purpose
wavers. A clocktower which locals
never check. A Gospel Hall where
seven old souls prepare for glory.

*

The moon? Here it is. A daily fix
of calcium above the castle, as if it
didn't also hawk over Pamplona,
the minnow Hebrides, Coimbra.

*

My hell somewhat less private than
yours, burning on YouTube, where
you merely redden, awkward with
your Sunday voice, newsreader face.

*

Alonzi's Harbour Bar, ices *in a dish*
and waitresses in lemon garb, their
overalls betraying weekday smalls
as I, spooning, am also see-through.

*

Teddy pickers front empty arcades;
dusk. Gull-carpeted sea, nausea for
Lynmouth, Weymouth, home, before
I resigned you to your compulsions.

*

So they buried Anne Brontë here,
but it was sister Charlotte said the
sea in any mood would satisfy her,
I shall be discontented at nothing.

A Small Photograph of the World Changing

Sorry didn't used to be an easy word; we screwed
our fists, we counted ten, rightly loath to say it.
Now it flies from our mouths; near strangers
pass notes with that single word penned in red.
We love too easily and it tails and scuppers us.
We forgive too easy and we become unpeople.

The ones I worry most for are those who say
they most fear losing worry's touch: one writes
what hurts is being loved too well, another is
sick with the thought of another year of waking,
solved and happy. It seems they feel such things,
they bear such things. They write them down.

Long before I forgave you, which can never happen,
long before I loved you easy, which I never did,
I found at the pit of your bag, down in the plunder,
a small snap which made the world drop through me
and I was a piglet who at last understood words
and petting me you said, *you're a silly baby I can eat.*

Bella

From the sperm whale's lampless throat
to the creamy throat of the coquette
in fourteen frothy months, half spent
rising through the sea's grim vault

and nodding in to the tideline – ambergris –
half spent negotiated, haggled over,
sealed in camphored oil, cobalt canister,
scentmaker's safe, sliced and finessed,

given over to the bonfire task
of making me lean in to you, all zeal
and trembling imperceptibly.
You smell amazing, bonnie girl.

*

Hot Meals Our Speciality. And so the cartoon chef
(moustache, puff hat) holds out the steaming plate
above an unseen customer.
Night might sway to fetish or flash flood

and, all hope, I am far out on the west
of my own rumour.
What do I hold over you? Nothing of harm,
or of power though. Not the beacon of flames,

to mimic the sun,
which Lord Shield Jaguar holds as Lady Xoc,
long face tilted to the light, draws the thorned rope
down through her tongue.

*

41

Things still here: first and final drafts, depictions
of the rare *dogtopus*; a torn slip where we'd shown
how we might sign our names; overnight sensations:
toothbrush, hairgrip, underwear and here,

a pale green ribbon, once twisted on your wrist,
by which one night I led you home. I've heard it say
you drown in three inches, and here I am. Unlost,
the terms by which I knew you: The Princess of Burma,

Hostage, Mermaid, Welcomed One, names now charted
which will not show up on the wider map,
abandoned towns you will not revisit,
where milkshakes sour and signs creak in the wind.

*

And then that afternoon you drew me in
among the crowds at Borough Market
and saw me near faint from some primal fear,
leading me out by the hand. I almost thought

to call you Daddy as, once or twice, with
a not wholly convincing wink, you'd done to me.
Haphephobia. The night we first kissed,
on the corner of the Terrace, you thought me

reluctant. That was not a lack of want.
It was the first sensing of the hard truths
we would learn from one another once I let you
close and the crowd of sweet hopes parted.

*

42

Rewalking this journey of just weeks ago,
from Village gelateria to the Heath's end then out
across that green spread pond towards The Hare,
where near chance first paired us, a route measured

by a waning ruby sorbet (fruitti di bosco, you would
approve, albeit you do not care for coloured stones
so the agate I fancied would suit your throat
stayed put on plush), since each ploughed route earns

eventual extent and so is measured: the coffin path
by the bearers' endeavour, each lush sea lane docked
by the coming shore, the giddily flawless circle
by its want of a starting point, or of a being sure.

*

The potboy's tremble as he stares down
the beauteous tea rose. The braggard's wince
as he heaves and anticipates the losing
of a little toe, his consequence of folly.

How the weak become the dead, and what
we store or invent: luck, is it, or backgammon;
what fills the little hours and I could list
and list and *have* to stop? Or I see you

close or have to dive for you. Easter Sunday.
On Creek Road, where your parents live,
a lively winter crimping spring, winter
dragging its chains, spring bringing itches.

*

Or if I think, yes, or if I think too much
'if I think' and end up at thinking
it's a nosebleed in a blizzard or, or
the cuppy smell at the end of things,

the dinge, the harmorama of holding
to the brittle thought. Think. Of. I'd sleep.
But best to sort. Boysy. X setting
his toy train to the track, Y parading

his stats on the web. I'm stuffed, Bella,
since no one is calling me wind chime,
since no one is telling me bald eagle,
so I lean into what's left of unholy night.

*

Tradescantia thrives in a bunged bulge flask,
myself not quite blissing but alive; you
in the lakes, not chatting, spring broken
from its dumbfounded nut, hallelujah,

that's a state of play. And am I happy?
Sitting where we met, brewing there?
Never happy Bella, did you notice?
The pond being a pond revolves, involves.

And who would not scorn the boy
who points out the tunnel at the end
of the light, who reads 'Hail Satan'
when the label, as so, reads 'All Satin'?

*

Love not enough? Last night my body
put me to sleep, then this morning,
a colleague's cancer, another's bereavement
to dwell on. Drawn to your youth?

Well, yes. You do not want the close-up shot
age shows you. They say you don't see black
just second guess the probables within the lack.
The drag to Waterloo disconsolates me;

the steps from Waterloo disconsolate me.
The library's a sump or morgue. I know
in any system there is Bella or honey.
But, drawn, dwell. Oh, love's not enough.

*

Soaked to want (unwritten in the stars).
The snows of spring bite the Hare Krishna
gaggle on Charing Cross Road, dis-eased boys
who will sheep back to suburban mothers.

A famous dancer leaves the bar; 'True Faith'
then 'Another Girl, Another Planet'.
My new self promise: not to treat you
like a child. And in the art deco mirror

I dab my new-cut hair. Not want, desire.
Then 'Going Underground'. Then humble,
then all that happened. Or us, sly and shy
on the Heath. Not knowing and not knowing.

*

Or us, in Greenwich Park. Two years on.
And me candyflossing, weepy – sorry, Bella.
Big chat. Then our usual pun and banter
and all sweetens. Sun and saunter to the Heath

where we cling and part. Cling and part,
yes, that was us. And your bob and wink
and your denk logic and your mellow tones
and your Jeanne d'Arc little sister, arms high.

One night, we fled the rainstorm, scarpering
on Bennett Park, soaked through with our laughter.
And love dried and tried us. We sought corners.
When I said always, what I mean is always.

Farewell to Couscous

I peered at the fancy buffet then rolled up my sleeves
but only to show my tattoos.

I was beavering beneath the surface of the archetype
of my archetype.

I was thinking *yestre'en*, that yestre'en I had gathered my brows
to make mourning from grief.

Or I had docked my peerie boat in the Orient of further debate.
Where *does* the Orient begin, Barry? Trick or trooshlach.

Blossom was skiving down Tavistock Place.

I distrust devourers. Those as eat two eggs ought to know shame.

I noted that others had opted for a life different to mine.

I was avoiding reflective surfaces – knowing what age
and tears do.

Don't argue whether my eyes are blue-grey or grey-blue.
Call them duck egg.

I knew at heart the Orient begins where couscous ends.

I was wondering how thin I'd need to get before Dom
dropped his joke: *A diet cider for my slim friend!*

I was squeaming at ramekins of mayonnaise, Satan's spittle.

On Churchway, I considered whether I would ever hear
a Universal horn, like the wind blowing.

Not that I have tattoos – or sleeves.

The ducklings the Lord giveth are the ducklings the Lord taketh away.

I figured Machiavelli must not have come from the class whose currency is the split lip and the bloodied nose.

How long had I known couscous anyhow? A brief culinary romance, a one meal stand.

I needed to choose a capital and a flag for the breakaway republic of myself.

I asked ABJ for five minutes, so I could finish this.

I was aimed towards five spice flood. Ginger dominion. From Head of Steam to Red Hot heaven.

I thought of how seldom you see grey on a flag.

I had mentioned the blossom, but few saw its significance.

I was milking the word *kismet*. I was draining the concept of the *Untertapische* – the scriptwriter beneath the carpet.

His universal horn.

I leaned back and began to tell of the *whole dreadful business.*

I must stop repeating myself, I repeated to myself.

REDUCTIONS

Astolat

The Flemish mapmakers
whose stale eyes would brim
and quake and brim

in honour of their poster boy,
half-kneeling,
the globe to his back

which once had encompassed
the lamia who swept,
without consequence,

with frothing lids,
and Elaine, who mopped
her woe ten tapering days

with moonstung silk,
if bolts of silk, I could not say,
had reached as far as us.

Salep

Came forth sweetness;
on mornings before a current
spurs and wires are live

comes the *genuine hot orchid*
fit to steal the cold
from any digger's spade.

Hot ferment of dogstone flour,
rose-baited, cajoled by sugar,
history unturnable,

the strong urn being
the handcart's hub,
an eternal cherub prammed

and seething, or the true crux
of the peeling kiosk's
century-long slow opening.

Ichor

A thumbs down to piling on,
to the fist over fist
of little England's schwa,

its terrace *svarabhakti*,
a bawling pusher-in
you'd finger in the line-up.

I need *amrotos* (a word
the Greeks could not swallow,
so they pouted in a b

as in *b* for brought by doves,
b for blood of gods), short
so sweeter, for many of us

now may never die,
a cupped hand of it
to rinse my modern mouth.

Comedo

Or you might see this
as a clamped molluscette
with one black foot when you

behold yourself, held reflected,
as you gaze into the memory
of stripling shame, all doors

locked, as your reflection now
rises from the pint of boiled,
salted water where you steep

and leech your witch's finger,
trails of pus like cooked egg
or strands of scat we'd squeeze,

harbourside, from hooked saithe
which had shoaled in
from the unreducing sea.

Taglion

An unpleasantry, an offputting
task you're putting off,
a close magic routine

which will cost a month
of practice. The trick
is to define and then divine

the sky, then point to it,
your twitch rods crossing;
your head high and tummy full

with copious yolk
and gummy, spiriting glair,
good water will rise up a well,

and righted, and
the dark time done,
you stand in air, on air.

Elmer

The soul as icky tincture,
a *drop in the ocean*,
a witch's swim bladder;

one monk's hang glide fills
an eleventh century myth,
beery breath in a balloon

sent counting up then down
the stacked floors of record;
a Le Quebrada diver's

few perilous seconds
to the welcoming gulch;
the nut of chemical honey

a bath pearl proffers between
my knees as I rehearse the role
of old soul, all soul.

Aello

A heatwave of burly days
and the slow stream rusts
and curdles to sour chocolate.

This mudpuppy
who has belted in and sunk,
stifle-high and yelping,

is the first, by alphabet,
of Actaeon's hounds,
while Tigris, the last, pants

blithe on the pale-grassed
brink, punishing a stick,
her good-name-given stuck,

or so I figure,
towelling my downy belly
after a cool shower.

Pardeur

After treatless months, fed
plain by a farmer neighbour,
the robber kitten

thinks me a new god, pushes
above, below my magazine,
for nibs of shortcake. Outside,

a sheep slurps slush
from an ornamental urn
from which she will conjure

bottlesworths of bottle green,
not quite the meaty piss
of lionesses who make stock

of the waterhole, or a wildcat's
spritzer lacing the curious
depths of Loch Wherever.

Agrodolce

The flaw in the fantasy's plot
which throws you off
the plateau phase

is there too in the elixir
as an acrid jolt
which the elixir masks

without which it would stay
unmixed, unswigged;
one utterance from

sweet silent space,
bitter from the lung,
not every trip's a holiday.

You know
that she would never
touch herself that way.

Kicap

Feeling positively groomed,
seeing the 'man in the moon',
fullest of counted moons,

feeling he ought to trim
that moustache that strays
rightward, to wipe

that grey sauce from his mouth,
too weary to check sense;
whether, on the other side,

dalliers might now spy
on some monochrome
girl who needs to hanky out

and mop her suppery lips,
so draining in one sweep
the Mare Ingenii.

Tragelaph

Precisions stalk
imprecisions, much as
purities steeplechase

impurities in the day's
olympic alembic,
elaborating the tincture,

that trusty servant
which will lock my mouth,
turn me half this half that.

To be precise, it's you
that I love still,
so now that lonely,

brindled lad the sitatunga
breaks the swamp's surface,
nose to the coming dusk.

Pulegone

What am I still into?
Knowing I grow so slowly,
that summer is coming,

and time – *only another liar* –
will try to hide the wall
where wallflowers thrive.

That, and the squall
of soft-loud-soft,
the catmint of mismelody

for which I'll drool and roll.
That, and luckless girls
of sulky appetite

who'd write my story
in their wombs,
their picas brimming.

Bouilli

In your play, which is called
The Lemon Tree,
a lemon tree must appear

eventually, just as,
in the room of typewriters,
the monkeys must hit

their one in 10^{900m} chance
of rewriting it. Much as,
when the run gives way,

a hand will pluck and juice
the fruit, reduce,
boil down the plot to sauce

then sit to eat, as the theatre
(*the stage outlives the play*)
sits through its dark week.

Colchis

Since still we shudder
when the snake hauls us
eye to simpler eye

and even our own vomit
sickens us to vomit,
we ache to turn

the timer full of sand,
to know gold and to learn
this I may eat, this

I might sip, or to stand
hard to the window
for the colours of the sky,

to know the colours
of what we may have been
or what we might yet win.

Ubald

Anything, I see now,
is the least nourishing slice
of everything. The seeming

sadness of unblocking
the kitchen sink is merely
the sadness within us,

which rolls at a constant
degree, infects the thinning
crowd of allies.

When they exhumed
the saint, they found only
an inch of oily liquid

into which each capitulant
dipped one wary finger, yet
their lives went unsatisfied.

Amygdala

This pack went higher
than jack, queen, king, by
seven strata of nobility, then

the tear-stung joker (the folly
of zero being absolute),
face a picture. After a game,

it was stored in a pearly jelly,
petrolatum or oil of almond,
the sort you'd use to gloss

the torso of a purring girl,
back when, or keep at bay
the soft chip of lithium,

a demented pet, its ambition
to leap the beaker's lip
and seed a storm of flame.

Bouvet

Peeled and gutted, the octopus
is dropped into the stock pot,
her last dip and mooch.

Or the invisible bones
of sundry shellfish invoke
the kitchen's fleshy weather.

With only six seas in us,
we must invent the holy pond,
the lonesome seventh,

that we might breast stroke
goggled and goose-bound
toward the farthest land,

the handsome ship
we dived from waning,
distant in a crystal wake.

Aarne

'Other Stories about Women',
perchance including
that one about my mother

as a girl, scoffing a whole
tin of condensed milk
and turning green.

'Mothers and Milk':
an unclassified motif,
a tale whose only catch

is the infant's latching on,
the cavegirl's wince
as she fumbles and fusses

the downy cherub
whose story now begins
as the campfire hisses.

Farewell to Conchiglie

(Eype – West Bay – Eype)

I most feared being asked what I most wanted.

I stood on the bar bridge and looked up the Lyme river.

A combo jazzed out one of one too many songs named 'You Belong to Me'.

I knew you could have minestrone without the pasta (but turn up that white pepper).

I thought of Kona, unable to speak her name in Portugal.

I roamed slit-eyed past huts selling cones of chips and cones of ice cream.

There was rye in my stomach and it was touch and go.

Three good things: a skipper butterfly, a tub of brown shrimps and a kissing gate.

Weymouth was hazy and behind me, if you see what I mean.

Such distance is neverending, neverending.

I was fairly sure I would die without jet-skiing.

I wanted to patent shingle walking as a remedy for gout.

I misted over when people talked of novels, or movies, or other assorted fictions, or me.

I climbed the steepness until it steeped the other way.

I thought of Charlie also steeping in the sun, slowly going the colour of my *Fab India* shirt.

And my friends weekending in Biarritz, Dom sharing with Al because he was *less grubby* than Nick or Gerard.

A boy made of his hands a neverending ladder for a ladybird.

And there ahead, at Sevelons, was Annie, perhaps with another 'good rope story' ready.

Her father's self-portraits were on the cover of every broadsheet.

Another father was teaching his young son to piss with the wind.

Three bad things: a fierce rabbit skull, a charred log, gnat legs jolting on my Factor 15ed nape.

Not that people talked often of me in my presence.

I was a lord of the flies and now I'd blown the conch.

I never cared for pasta anyway. My failure to admit that is to my shame.

I sent a shock of water down into my well.

Piss with the wind? Frankly I didn't give a damn.

Old local proverb: *on a shingle strand there are no shells.* Its meaning lost in time.

Some times there are no pros and cons, just cons and cons.

But I did give a damn. I always had.

DOUBT VERSUS HOPE

Doubt

One night, when sleep would not
knock back in and the bills were unpaid,
I lay in the pearl light and my body
was lukewarm and I thought of kissing you

on a roof or you sitting on my knee and people
knowing at last that we were something
but you were a borough away and I was not
allowed you since you were young and I

was not and I sought some tiny hope
in the curtain's chink or the bark of something
distant, familiar yearns, but it was doubt
I sensed, sculling the room with its long oars.

Halfway Through the Year of the Rabbit

Omnes hore vulnerant

Yes, a notion of light left in the sky.
Which small pleasures remain but those
surfacing in the standfast law of routine?

Night. I am becoming used to the music,
to the music of this, its struck carillon,
its rosalia of blunder, muddle, gaffe.

I sit in hope for a day that resembles
someone I like. Too often now I'm clean
but used. My yesses are hatching as nos.

I'd sing a lullaby, to which I'd knock
my ancient staff; my thoughts are only
the rick-rack things guests leave in a bothy.

Unsudden pleasures are the room's light,
fur soft, the stack's thrum, the library
of other oddball's inner yells and yawns.

No room at the inn of plenty. No belling
of the stag of 'make it so'. The lark
might rise supreme, which will not happen.

What track is this? Ah, that paramount
of minimalism, silence: slayer of thiscore
and thatcore, queller of downtown music.

If I could learn its pitch, to shrug down
the nipping annoyances, to unhook love's
dandy cape, not to cast this shifty umbra.

69

Still dawn as far from me as distant suns
or the colossal amours of others. I can't
imagine the morning's flimsy ballerinaing.

Eight hours ahead, the Rabbit, in truth
a Hare, hurdles over the breathy music
of the grass, chasing needs, chasing itself.

Or it chases a train which frisks up the edge
of the slowest of rivers, its eyes pale stones
from that silty fathom. I might yet blossom.

I set the needle down onto another fugue
of silence. My longing brims and spills.
I sense this train could travel either way.

Bad Players

Halfway down the carriage, the cackling girl,
too loud for my introspective sensibilities,
turns out to be a bloke, someone Stoke City
might have let go, free transfer, circa 1980.
I think of the girl swimmer who rouses herself
at 6am, to knock through two hundred lengths,
but behind her back, her nickname is 'Seventh'.
I want to hug those who make the semis, those
who dream on, those who reach county stage,
hit the under 21s then flood away. You triers,
you are okay, even decent, but you do flail
when the proper people nail you. Sorry, losers.
I am nothing much but I go for what I go for
because life has only offered me that much.
At the tail end. The senior circuit. Do you see
hills dipping through mist, dead legs, bullies
tipping something you loved into the lake?
You got to the last stage of the interview?
And now it's a balcony and the glass of wine
and the ciggy, which tastes vile, to the taste
of one who wins. We are quite content
to put 'quarter-finalist' on your headstone,
okay about patting you and saying, softly,
'you did quite well'. Come over, I am open
to talking this with you, I am only part winner,
I have been there in the suburb of all discontent.
My heart has been dubby. I have at times, oh,
at times, screwed. I look at you, bad players,
and think of time I have spent on my own,
the sad walk to hope. And now you are
out for a duck, taken off at half time. Your
Olympic dream remains a dream. Bad player.

Late light on the pitch calls you on and you
and, horror, I are going nowhere and we know
it's over. Heroes, we were something once.

All You Philosophers

who know the thing about two fingers in the river
know also about the way the river does not rise
in the mind's sync. You have persuasioned the river
and known its has is has. You have occasioned
perhaps another river and dimmed it to find
its river essence is other. You know the river
settles for you, if you dream best. That if the river
broaches, it will skim in your best morning dream.
Any river kisses you, for they are easy. You reckon?
A river arrives on the scent skills of my masters,
me being not-philosopher, and it rubs and goes.
If it were Tuesday, I would run down on thoughts
on rivers, but these are the early hours of Saturday
and a river is gunning through what I think of
as my house. The river has two edges, the river
coaxes to completion, these guesses are beyond guess.
The river as philosophy is the book I've not written,
okay, or read, but I can see it, sense its only scope.
Rivers and beasts are easy, they hum with all
that childhood left me. Philosophy loses rivers.
I have tried, but I am limited. I meet the grand ones.
But rivers slim by. I have not dived into one.
Casual sex happens by them, as does raucous noise.
The elements, which are among my trusted friends,
tell me rivers, but doubt, which is my harmony,
speaks that all that we say of rivers is nothing much,
is the empty in a pyramid, is the empty in a skull.

Towns You Only Pass Through

Their systems linger, awaiting your arrival,
which will not happen. We zip, we air gun,
and we do not stop. Windygates, Kenilworth,
I see your Co-ops, your lonely ironmongeries,
your tangle of lanes I might possibly dally in.
Chesterfield, I doubt we will ever meet proper.
Yet a newsagent sign catches my eye, a woman
bent to some task of thought. On a wet corner
in Barnstaple, a vicar and a poppet bat a balloon.
It is green and always must be. Gary, Indiana,
proving this is everywhere, or some grey town
south of St Malo, where we did not stop to buy
beef for that chilli or a basket of cold beers.
Newark and Stevenage, fetish settlements
for the passer through, each with its microcosm
of neverness, model villages helium pumped
till bachelors and long lost women parade
their shadowier provinces, seeking orange juice
or scourers or the last paper plates in the store.
Make my point? Oh, it is that there is not one.
I grew to what I am in a town you can never
pass through, unless you are driving into the sea.
Passing through is ever a sort of phobia, a fear
that the lethal or panic might happen anywhere
and best to move to destination. Arrival
is always the better of it. You clasp your sides
and stretch, you ready. What would come
is simmering with value, it will tie you
in its maze of desperate but needful inevitability.
Gort, with your Brazilians and your meat;
Salem, Oregon, not even the frightfullest Salem;
Stara Pazova, an instant gush of the 1950s, now.
I will get over you, by which I mean so many things.

I might run through you, crowing 'not for me',
I might mention you in passing, boredly, probably
only to myself. You are not worth the sleep
I might lose. But cannot lose. Northampton, bless,
some lazy morning I will drive through you
in a souped-up Bentley I cannot even drive.
And my dear heart will burst with the awfulness
of reaching your shrubby limits, of carrying on.

Tact

Mid-afternoon and I enact a policy, the elementary one against ambiguity. So, in this park, it's simple beasts at first: a squirrel is a sculpted pigling, nut in mouth; a cinnamon-headed fly romps on a slab; a blackbird scraiks in the hedgerow, delving reddest berries, ones which tease from me the giddy painters' words for scarlets; a toadstool, stillest of brutes, stirs uncautious concepts – the prettier of two sisters, or the prettily filmy phases of a bruise (tact is not yet ambiguity). Then, wild coriander (the local word a cheekful of hornets), a violet lozenge of a butterfly, and another an inch off lemon. And at last, what was missing from your bestiary: a grey-bellied rodent flossing the old teeth of a dry wall; new lovers who laugh at they don't know what; some cousin of the waxwing which halves the space between maple and beech, heads to where policy and concept meld or melt, to the self's sluice, where it settles to drink.

Jambhala's Mongoose

spits jewels from its pretty mouth
to show it is not its cussed little enemy
the snake, whose poltrooning odyssey
across continents, through gluey seas,
threading the high canopy, plunging
through scrub and shale and scree,
is learned of just after we learn
to approach the nipple, talk, to lie;

is every thing of hope to the serpent's
cowl of doubt; walks southward,
westward, the directions of the blood,
filches, pelters, mimics lazy rain, since
all is well, in tow with natural law, bows
to the protector's moony throne, nods
to the gammadion, slinks his limbs,
his *fower-fot*, a pelty tetraskele;

prefers the skiff of pleasure
to that hanger and flogger, love,
shoots down alleys, rubs its belly
on stones warmed by the only sun it knows,
gains a mossy wall, basks on a shed roof,
on the day's ardent pall, fails to tally
who, of all its allies, it will never
clink with, never meet again.

Fear of Lions

Q: Where does a lion go to sleep?
A: Wherever he wants.

At least I know now that I will never take charge
of the master ship, ploughing the sounds
around an undiscovered continent,
Good Hope unrequited, unrequired,
turning the great wheel with my elbows,
in inch thick blindfold, to give the task
more bustle. No admiral then, no swinging anchor,
more a quaking, melancholy anchorite.
My saintly attributes will be these:
a nightingale clinging to my dowdy epaulette,
a disc-faced owlet, dunked in the bolehole
of my new-sprouted willow. And together
we will battle our fear of lions,
those gaspy boys, those slick girls cantering
through head-high grass, needy
to gift us to their bellies, so the charm of sleep,
the slumberlust, might start.

Fantigue

How whistle thrash bids tempests roar
WALTER SCOTT, 'Rokeby'

I am the one for sorrow, dipped
out from the shoal, without leave,
both a boy who flipped the mabinogi
and this biddy caitiff, aimless,
checking the dubby sky for hope.

If I dream of the lucivee, her claws
bunked in my back, it mustn't mean
the praying mantis won't hear my yaps
with its only ear, but I will thick my blood
with whistling, its gory truth, tomorrow.

Solutomaattimittaamotulos

The newsagents, and a man teaching his small son about the palindrome. Madam, I'm Adam. *Other forms were near.* My head was clicking between the end of Joyce's 'The Dead' and the two sides of an old single by Grace Jones – 'The Apple Stretching' and 'Nipple to the Bottle', the latter of which I fashioned I could appropriate, it being not property of any brittle sort. I can name you six songs about female down and outs. Bag ladies. Bench sitters, like Marie, crammed by a cement truck by the Tea Hut a year back. *The Times / Mumsnet* crossover tells me to put courgette in my frittata. Tomato is in the middle of nothing really when you take the time to consider. There are few responsible laboratories. *Keep the lid on, I'm still a lady.* I reconnected with my mother today. Time refuses the standing still offered by idiom. I worry on the middle letter of a palindrome, its wall-flower *angst. The air of the room chilled my shoulders.* I think of the girl in the lane. There are times at night I listen to the lighted windows I can see from the balcony and wonder if others worry. Others worry.

A Mixed Grill

Bug-eyed, I see the platter off, its dozen components
motley, a carousel of savoury, undignified, and not
themselves, bringing to mind Sherbrooke, Quebec,

those pubescent girls I'm reading of, at an end
of term party lushed into trance by a novice hypno
who had not yet learned how to bring them back;

one's gluey ear hard to a trestle, another stiff
in her first polka dots, a third girl sliding off
her chair at an inch per minute, a far star dipping

a distance from the heart unfathomable, unbearable
as this photograph, when I turn the page, of
a 'jar of preserved moles' which I am gaping at:

a crammed cosmos of inexistence,
a jamboree of snout, pelt and not a direction
in heaven not pointed at by a sprig of bone.

Mostly in my life I have been me
and when I dig, I dig towards the light
and in that solemn system of returning, I return.

Halfway Through the Year of the Dragon

She loves the music box forever, she's crying on my shoulder
THE BLUE NILE, 'Stay'

You can mythologise anywhere but you cannot
                              romanticise it,
or anyone. You hear the song. You know this:
                    the girl is Moira,
not Lolita and it's a scrappy rowan at best
                        not a lemon tree.
Women are mean… and snakelike,
                    my flatmate proposes,
from the next room. It's the top of summer,
                    but we are both
too existential to even open the balcony door.
                    A long pause,
then she adds, *Except for me, I am humble.*
                    Some masters
painted the serpent with the face of a woman.
                    When he sings
of the parade, you sense it's only the Byres Road,
                    that the hiss and talk
is of football (not *saudade*, not the Dreamtime
                    and for sure it's not
the flinty, mighty dream time of the rénchén).
                    His gritty tinseltown
cranks up, the spotlit fountain huffs blue rain.
                    And this, this con,
this chicanery we pull, descendant of alchemy,
                    is what we do:
play musk, play magic into the sipping dusk,
                    dragon into the humble,
unsure where the snake, all myth and no romance,
                    will find its level.

Poem in Which I Stand Next to an Emperor

The sovereign gadge sports orangey brown
which serves his ginger, lukewarm stance
and languid poise, his numbered months.

The sun beyond us shifty in exceptional blue,
the weather holds. We hold this pose, just so,
as a rumpussing kitten holds tight to a moth.

My skewy, somewhat thumbs-up suggests
the gatefold inner sleeve of a farewell album,
its rowdy anthems slowed to heaven speed.

Goodbye John

You can't reach my age without having wanted an alley named after you and one evening I had found myself staring into Prince of Orange Lane, far from fit for a prince, a short, dark slice of Greenwich leading to a boarded gateway and I'd wondered if I might have it retitled, thinking none of the princes and marquises who now contest the title would miss it, too drawn by the strings of their nobility to even catch wind. I had moved to a favoured grill dive, where the hot sauce is danger red, then hailed a jaunty cabbie who didn't wrinkle when I said only, 'take me up to The Village?' This was around the time when the Finnish dancer and her forty dresses had moved into the back room, and I was spinning Calvinistically from anthology to anthology, before *The Guardian* called me 'ubiquitous' and things unspooled. A time of continued nausea but cautious buoyancy. We had taken to promising each Wednesday after class not to end up in the stinkpit which served stiffly priced drinks halfway to dawn, but weekly there was a weakening, and we'd strut from The Pineapple, pretending there was an alternative, bleakly denying we were in a soapbox cart and at the bottom of this steepest moral hill was Da Vinci's, where we'd huddle in the odd light till the eerie became seductive, our faces phasing to sweet and sleepy, and watch couples who were clearly married but not to each other, coming to honour the turned down TV showing kick flicks and the bad garage bursting and John and I would listen mostly to the women, that being the best of things, as we burnt the hours we could not afford, all talking over this awful art our fussed amygdalas had pulled us down into, till the night turned us into plots of perfect sickie calls and sherbets south and Eloise could cross off one more of the sofas of London. I'm fairly sure this was the week I received a Valentine's card, from a cat. A male cat, though somewhat feminine in appearance. A card which had been prompted by heavy hinting in after midnight texts to the owner (here, pity pity), a woman I needed more as a friend than as anything more, though it stung like an unnamed alley to compute that. I had recently read and noted that, 'There is no physical law that prevents time travel' and I passed the short walks between home and Village in putative De Loreans, Tardises, bedisked chariots, thinking to witness the Sermon on the Mount, the last stumble of the last unicorn and the cat, climbing the pillar box to post the card, the envelope raspily licked and kissed.

Unknown Pleasures

Thin and twenty and having a suitably lousy day,
so her face instructs me, she wears the iconic logo
on her shirt, perhaps unaware it's pulsar CP1919,
its radio waves bristling.
                            Across the carriage,
two young girls are embossed in binary attitudes
of absorption: one perlustrates the ingredients
of her Lush strawberries and cream soap;
the smaller one leafs the final pages of her book,
Pompeii, with a dingy look, till she reaches
the endpapers, indigo.
                            I'd guess the brain contains
both the nest and the egg, that sweetest water
some days rolls free from the rustiest of taps.

Miss Martindale in the Outback

The Royal Mail Hotel refuses to be verbed.
It does not squat and it will not loiter,
it baffles each challenge, announces
'call me a bastard of a newish nation',
'a sump of heat and brigand nerve'.
It swiffs between a tight lack of shadow
and impossible shadows which point lazily
and longly towards an imaginal sea.

There are no jackdaws, minimal chess
is apparent. This is a town she would not
walk out of, sun-bright, with catharsis
guddling her rainless tongue. Tea rose,
beagle and rockpool drain from memory.
The sky is a monstrous itch, the very blue
of hunger or the super blue of desire.
Rocks scowl, rocks impersonate the real.

There is moving and there is the moment.
The out. The back. Even if pleasure descends,
a home away from home, then anyone
might stand at this brink, this fugitive nub
with occasional trains and improbable rain,
seeing, now that hope grips a shoulder
with a lenient hand, that the one way out
is the fair twin of the way in: to choose it.

Tranquil Vale

How I like these occasional characters in this soap,
Village People, in which I think I star. Lora, say,
who lights up any screen she appears on, or, yes,
the men of the Conroy dynasty. Those who cameo,
so deliciously, who walk on and off, who enrich.
The exes who offer a drumbeat moment – Laura
at The Crown's door; someone saying softly,
is that Catherine? Andy Swift has a line now and then,
dapper and content with his age. Brian walks his lab
down the hill, Tash sorts Sam, Eugene will turn up
in the pond one day, we are sure. Sophie will arrive
from Paris, Mil will come to the quiz, still a little
in love with Jason Donovan. Toby walks the Vale
in a coat I could not afford. Mark's moped muttonchops.
Who was the girl at Morden's who every man sighed for?
The directors are writing this in for effect, but I sense
affect, that dangerous aftershave of an emotion. I see
Charade walk in, no longer a major character, or Simon,
who leaves early and we suspect has a spin-off crime series,
or Maddy, who we all know wears stockings. Hedley
knows us, The Crusader knows us. There are people
who give us our names, who endanger us with names,
our lovers wilting in the greenhouse blackness of love,
our parents thinking maybe we will squeeze one more.

Lines on a Young Lady's Facebook Album

Unsauced, unseated and on the wrong timeship
to be other than an axed part in your maybe show,
yet my numbed and thudded fingers find the grip
on the eye of a needle I thumbed in some years ago.

The darkest eyes. I watch them scroll through screens,
your fingertips enlarging some young man
you're doting on. Misfortune hogs such scenes.
Old men have suffered so since men began.

The Last Hour of Her Teens

What can't we give away? What of the the heart's
exubera, the plot's inky detritus? Some talk perhaps

of the heart? Surprise us. Explain that unfathomed
graze, that tear stain on a cheek. Now she has time

for one last prank call, five sambuca shots before
the hour will ring time on the lily and wildfire

of pure youth. So all are circling the famous sins,
shaking afraid, waiting for their lines. On far oceans

ships tilt, dark at the belly, yellow decklights
barely worrying the foam; in forests and in deserts

shy beasts quirk their snouts toward the wind, sense
tough verbs in the sentences of themselves,

angling for what has changed, what heart to heart.
We make the dancefloor move, play our parts

imperfectly. No one stops to say, 'what were we?'
Eyes in the house of night. And Francesca twenty.

Brutal

The waiter sets down in front of her
his bowl of chicken Caesar

and for the man
her steak still frothing on the bone.

He has been served
the one rock Lochnagar Reserve

while she now has
his large glass of Shiraz,

too sweet and hissy. Forgivable errors:
mixing up Berlin and Porter

or cumulus and cirrus,
triceratops and stegosaurus.

First time someone thought you my daughter,
I reached for clearer things: tap water,

leather, grape pips. Et tu.
The couple exchange plates. Of course they do.

Halfway Through the Year of the Snake

What did winter ever let us do but find edges:
some we could skiff off, some we'd cook and eat.
By summer we had found music, of sorts:
music heard along the beach, also the brash songs

of things snagged in traps. My head went south
to romance, its circusy brilliantine or deft art
of harm. I wanted. Cuss and cant were sweetening.
I sensed some essence. Wanted double cream,

rapture, absolute; did not want a cordon on value,
did not want more than one response. Others,
I knew, parsed or skimmed the day, saw sparrows
as sparrows skiffing the greenery. Not all honey.

Again I prowled the thought of whatever season's
finespun rig-ups. A snake cannot force a home
from a house of cards; its zigzaggish hatchling
would spatter a marmalade blush light bulb.

Yet I didn't clamour for any home, saw stink-hard
through its yammy appeal. Music, I told those
who did not ask, was all of seduction and charm,
the most fine of the small and acceptable seas.

The skim, notice, is not being ample for delicacy.
The sea, too soon a nook to weep in. I fathomed
the ingredients for happy within me. I fashioned
an empty sack, willing to walk to any beginning.

Farewell to Dumplings

Danube Strand, Novi Sad

I was off.

I had entered the lands of the eagle, of the bear, of the
eagle-and-the-bear.

I wrote down 'a horse and cart is more or less a centaur'.

I wrote 'what looks like smoke on the horizon', then corrected
that to 'smoke on the horizon'.

Mid-afternoon and I veer toward the bridge. Роди. Radi.

I swot the international language of the magpie, of floristry,
the international language of the crotch.

I recall the mantra, 'write what you hear, say what you see'.

The eyes are drawn to a squeal of brakes, to a squall of coffee.

To the bridge!

The Danube was floating a rosebud, was drowning ants.

Every stone kicked or stick thrown changes our world, or so I think.

The eyes are drawn to texting drivers, indoor smokers, to a poet
accepting a prize, in *trainers*.

In the shadier nooks of the strand I practise a smile – too old to
learn.

Better (just) to praise a small nation than to dispraise.

I was all but new to the lands of the double-headed eagle, the
double-fisted bear.

I checked my preparatory vocab from Vedrana: *Thank You,
Good Day, Cheers, Good Music, Yes, Beer, No, Ajvar.*

The Drunken Clock looms from the fortress river-over.

I practise *Da li y ovome ima pšeničnih sastojaka (brašno itd)?*
Does this contain wheat products (flour etc)?

For wheat grows in any new garden, Novi Sad.

Now Sade climbs the basement bar steps onto Newlyweds Square.

Jer ne smem to da jedem. Because I cannot eat them.

The Jelen stag bells its latest bell.

Now Metallica follow Sade up those steps. A quid a beer.

But I can't resist the dumplings which come with Zoe's goulash.
I inhale half of one, like a dying gangster at his last cigar.

Farewell slim dictionary language of clootie dumpling,
minority language of har gau, dead language of tortellini.

I weigh the hotel's 'fading elegance' against my own.

Maultaschen, manti, pantruca, karanji: I never knew you, girls
I did not kiss.

Sometimes I worry that every room I am not in contains a party.

A party at which I would think much and say little. I was born
like that.

THE BELLS OF HOPE

The Autist

A sweet, doomed saint
computing his aliquots – the divided self prefers pear and plum

and damson, self-sweetened entities – is this flat's sole megafaun,

stalking his quiet land for scare tales of dentist and hairdresser.

The Brunt

The period murderess,
ever less handsome than the actress who will play her.

Blame inching along the red brick lips of the koi pond.

Blame prying into each of a circle's thousand corners.

The Canon

It's Hemingway,
arisen, indignant, his hands at your throat. And Gogol, too close

behind you, hacking. It's Colette, twinning your motives. Beyond

the scut of doubt, day playing night, cred-siftingly badly, miscast.

The Disparity

Coincidence
and chance are siblings, but tracks that stretch in unpaired directions:

one courts the mind's sun as it falls on celandine hills and blockades

of wire and salt; the other yields to the sweetmeat lands of the body.

The Everafter

Bells for who?
Who will we ring for, from those we met on this crossing,

those wrung ones, our wrecked brethren, our seatown girls

scuttled or snagged in creaking ice, or air the shade of ice?

The Fathoming

As sorrowful
as a drawerful of damp grey bras, or a yes with a probably tacked on,

with peppery lips numb and heart doing closework, you are balanced

on the sill of wisdom, having grasped how few kind words are meant.

The Gladiator

True believing
is a flux of Enemy and Folly. So though you thumbed me, empress,

my ear is to hope, and I'll wade blind into this sword squad of blond

boys, aware no simple blade can satisfy what falls beyond condition.

The Hometown

I'd been a boy
but could not barani or shin up to the crest of the Maiden Rock.

And I could barely march, not even out into the cold sea where

a saint's kneecap and fingerbones bobbed in a tide-trapped cave.

The Interlude

A sort of race,
this holding on: a static march, bundling of constant thought.

An amphitheatre caught between cruel games and sightseers.

A town where we call the river a river though we see it's dry.

The Junction

Men redden from thought
and in the dayclothes of that thought stand on, where life

has placed them. There on that corner they scuff, musing

on the roughest of comforts, how for now it may suffice.

The Kismet

The Voice of God?
That sprat pulled from the south sea of thought. It may as well be

mine. Dahmer was God to his pounces. And me, so gamely douce,

as much a God to all I name, gesturing through the windowglass.

The Lothario

As quick to wake
as a boiled egg topped, you test the morning with one eye, find

her Elvisy boudoir and the sounds of her spooning gunpowder

tea into a pot. *Girl tax.* You lie there denying it, ambassadorial.

The Machine

An egg when cooked
is all tails. Wink into its one yellow eye and see

its spectre chick, a gibbet spirit, *uniquely broken*,

unable to sift the topfreeze for specks of summer.

The Nevermore

The awful heartwork
of it and that I'm saying, shamefully, aloud, here on the balcony

that I love you as if still there were a teasing plenty, when, when

teasing plenty is gone and that, *that*, beyond my stash of chance.

The Orient

All Greek?
Yet Greek is simple, cosy. A bird is a 'needlebeak', a plant a 'pinkbranch'.

It's we who complexicate. Add one hour of lingual restraint, each country

east, till the island where the only man whispers his name to the only tree.

The Preservation

A weekend's thoughts:
water voyaging across Europe, вода, wody, Wasser, uisge.

Then some fieldside ditch where it thickens to near-sense.

Alexander cooling in honey. Nelson scalp-deep in brandy.

The Quandary

On time and age
great wisdoms have entered near silence; itched heads begin to nod

to enemies unmatchable with wit and saw: so plaster lambs smile on

a butcher's shelf, a sign shows a happy cod handing us a fork, a knife.

The Razor

Your foglike sleep,
as if nothing happened in this room. I'll release the tortured boy

beneath the ten day beard of a gentleman of leisure. Play misty

for yourself. Even a path through the prettiest forest has an end.

The Shy

Grin and vie,
empty the barrels of your why, where, who, send cans skidding

off the garden wall, to roustabout the patient gardener beyond it

who trowels the shadowy rows in a mauve skirt and summer hat.

The Taster

Sour forgiveness,
carnival shame, all slosh in my tastevin of memoir raunch. The bath

is filling; the steam is however you connote sweet without writing it.

Here, on my chimaeric, inner canvas I daub your three salty mouths.

The Upturn

Your luck will change.
How high the lark might rise. You will make it to the feast's

last hour as the twite, never sorry for itself, canters on wind,

exhausting the day, a near nil of flesh. Flesh, wine and song.

The Valve

Not yes, not no,
the matter's heart lies in turning: with or against the clock? To

resolve might take the vocal scale of a plateau phase or a sharp,

storm scent of a someone entering some room. *Solfège. Orage.*

The Wobegone

The lift fills
with tiny, pale moths, drawn to what you know they are drawn to.

I blow them into the hallway and, entering, I wonder if this house

misses its child the way I miss you, my lost jaggy thistle of a bairn.

The Xerox

You remind him
and that's enough to saint you, and yet you sit there claiming there is

no shadow on you, though he discerns it, theatre curtain thick, even

on your slim thighs plaited in hubris. Ah, but a heart refuses to copy.

The Yore

So long ago
that the world still smelled of smoke and girls would reach their

cruel age quick. Uncommon then: an envelope stuck not tucked,

a shadow tailing and then flooding, a war heard through a wall.

The Zombie

Day will find you,
formed from blood pearls – staghorn sumac bobs surging –

surfaced in the tub of yourself, risen from the pit in which

you lay yourself, a head full of snake kings, full of snakes.

The Yen

Such caution
is as much of passion as I can marshal, though I could raise

a full cohort of doubts, readied at the edge of the battle site,

each with a power-washed cobble of a face, and a split lip.

The Ximenean

Some night will reveal
the colour of the lie, flood light the field where you fluked the latest

battle. Till then you adopt the compromise rules, sleep on the letters

never sent, lay the traces of the light. That proper character, a ticker.

The Winddown

This everything
is something about dying. This gallon heart misheard as galleon heart.

This boding. This gadding cause. This vibey scorn. This advice: *learn*

your best songs young. This, the body, its clock sorely needing wound.

The Verification

A handbell is jived
to summon the dwelling's full cast; all appear (malarial hero, lover

out to grass and doomed boy, home truth-seeking trinity) becoming

one on a hard chair, to make (sense of) this pareidolic declamation.

The Underfull

This real Midas,
his face painted and in his hand a hand: both jokers, then a prial

of queens by turn betokening speed of bounty, a heart of plenty,

and this shadow on me of you who once loved me. *Full House.*

The Treatment

Much as a brute
kisses the eyes which earlier he blacked, blots the peach-puffed cheeks

of his *Irish beauty*, two suns burning one another, I slip down capsules

of milk thistle, darling of all its tribe, my liver begging, a fat baby bird.

The Silence

As glue does,
the gloom sets on a sepia nude you know must now be dead,

on a century-old report of a double drowning at the headland.

Fat pads of felt stifle the tongues of the fabled bells of hope.

The Rendering

About as bad
as a couple who call each other 'baby' is this grim acceptance

of my long-held recognition that I am not one the holy camera

loves. The Lord preserveth. Vinegar beckons me. Aspic woos.

The Quizzers

Last aftermaths
of my youth thieved by heat from her young breast as she unsexually

leans in to read questions. Hours till dawn, when a man was shot for

lesser crimes than recognising himself in the faces of the firing squad.

The Puppet

Love is mere instinct;
our character is no less than the sum of flaws in the perfect peach

of the brain's blueprint, its brimming *taxis*. This hand in the glove

of us is clinical. It wears a second glove, cut from uncompromise.

The Oratorio

An air as fine
as any song is, slowed to a sole voice, or the sacred songs

of dimday grainsmen slow crossing meadows home, much

as the past and holidays *feel* traversing the amygdala's mirk.

The Nimbus

Sweet, then repeat
was all I ever learned. No song of my composing ever earned

a fourth chorus. Think *pig lamps* not *limelight*. Moving water

is the greatest art work. I loom, a raincloud of my former self.

The Musing

Such cowardice
to fear my demise, which I have so wanted. A slush of song,

your photographs, and shame a broth left zealing on the ring,

its oniony fragrance hiding the truth: the heart kills quickest.

The Longshot

Unlikely angling:
noble dosser seeks kitten, figurative or actual kitten, or kitten

as concept. If luck should open its only eye, or if plenty shows

its face, be sure to use the name given often, till she knows it.

The Kundalini

The meat was darker
when I was younger and sleeping. What ticked at the far edge

of my luck? That more of the meat was dark. Where my head

woke in the pillow was the magnetic centre of a subtle county.

The Jeater

The black I can work,
and work, manumitting troche and trait and spillikin from

the sable yield. And in the dark time shy as farwoods fungi,

right here where the forest is beginning to reclaim the field.

The Inclination

Unfond land,
the years. Between *left* and *gone*, a long, down gradient

to tug your shin strings, beef your calves. Until? Until

the memory of her wanting has no savour, and no smell.

The Haunt

Betwixt of January,
the year's scantest trawl. The sharking ghost of Anne Boleyn

would raise a shrug. But my ghost would void your bowel.

My ghost would hug you hard – then hug you far too hard.

The Gazer

Only that sky
was ever starry. There never was a starry hand-me-down,

a starry changeling. I return the glare of the waste of night,

my long watch expertly balanced between –ology and –ism.

The Flitter

Little chicane
torsoing on the toilet floor, a silverfish, a fellow sliver to my waddling

Villagewards in Platonic cinerama summoning the bounteous words

for 'little', not one of which will come, where you came, on my tongue.

The Epitome

Supposed friends
claim I would hang a sticky rack of sauced and frazzly ribs

on the thick night sky, as apogee, though I would not hang

my own, nor yours, though your kiss I silently recommend.

The Desiccation

Which sun dried
these sun-dried things? For its light must be Concorde cutlery

sharp, its heat that of a fine room in which a smell of buttered

toast intuitively arrives, as summer does on a rumoured coast.

The Corrida

Shadows not blood
on my quaking hand, supper smells from two rooms away (a *family* home)

and a far-off grumble, the hooves of Marengo or Bucephalus. Not taunting

but self-examination. Diagnosis: ripening towards the congruous unworld.

The Bore

I've kept on,
haven't I, muttering about both the sea and the sky, as if to do

so might mean that love was not a feast so moveable that it

seldom stops to let us point and tell each other what we saw?

The Approximation

The usual bores
tell me we are the only creatures who stare at the moon. I count

struts on the back wall of The Glebe until cold sends me in. We

thrive in cold. Perhaps you fallen angels disagree? Let me know.

GLOSSARY

Many of the poems in this book, especially the *Reductions* sequence, make use of unusual language, so I thought a glossary would be helpful and of interest.

Aarne: Finnish folklorist who categorised folk tales
Aello: one of Actaeon's hounds
agrodolce: a sweet and sour Italian sauce
amrotos: the word which became *ambrosia*, the 'b' sound added due to *svarabhakti* (see below)
amygdala: part of the brain associated with emotion and memory
Astolat: the castle of Elaine, as in 'The Lady of Shalott'
banderole: a flag or streamer, or a speech scroll on an old painting
bouilli: any boiled dish but sometimes a reduced sauce of a single fruit
Bouvet: the world's most distant island
caitiff: a coward or villain
calumet: a Native American 'peace pipe'
Colchis: the land where the Golden Fleece was kept
comedo: a blackhead
denk: a text message misspelling of 'drunk' which has become slang
dogstone: a former name for orchid tubers, ie dog's testicles, which they resemble
dragee: a small, hard sweet, often used to decorate cakes
Elmer: a monk who tried and succeeded in doing what we would now call hang-gliding
fantigue: agitation
gasconade: a daring boast
glair: egg-white
goose-bound: referring to the goose fat long distance swimmers sometimes use as insulation
haphephobia: a dislike of being touched, especially by people you do not know

kicap: the original word which became 'ketchup'

komakino: better known as a song title by Joy Division, it is a (perhaps putative) film genre

ichor: the golden blood of the Gods

ihana tanssija: Finnish for 'lovely dancer'

Irish beauty: old slang for a woman with two black eyes

jeater: a term for one who makes things from the organic mineral jet.

Kongzi: the general name in Chinese for the sage Confucius

lamia: mythic women who constantly wept

La Quebrada: a place in Mexico famous for its cliff diving

lucivee: an old name for the lynx

Mare Ingenii: the Sea of Cleverness, one of the few seas on the moon's 'dark side'

moi moi: Finnish for goodbye

myokymia: a muscular problem which causes a twitchy eye

naumachia: a staged gladiatorial battle at sea

nomicon: a debatable word which connotes either a book of laws or a list of names

Pardeur: a cat's name, word play from 'chat pardeur', from 'chapardeur', French slang for a thief

pica: a food craving, especially during pregnancy

plateau phase: the level of sexual pleasure preceding orgasm

pulegone: a substance found in catnip and pennyroyal (a plant associated with reproduction)

rénchén: this is the water dragon in the Chinese zodiac

rosalia: in music, a sequential modulation, a repetition of a passage in another key

saithe: a pilchard-like fish

salep: a rich, hot Turkish drink made from orchid flour

schwa: the neutral vowel, as in *England* when, as often, pronounced, Eng-uh-lund

scunnerations: Scots, annoyances

sitatunga: an antelope which sleeps below water for protection, with only the nose above surface

slow opening: the 'rehearsal' period before a restaurant properly opens *stillicidal:* relating to water falling regularly in drops

svarabhakti: the adding of a sound to a word to ease its pronunciation

taglion: the pointed end of an egg

teddy picker: an arcade game where you attempt to lift a prize out of a heap with a crane device

tragelaph: a fabulous beast, half-goat, half-stag

trooshlach: Scots, trivial nonsense

Ubald: the patron saint of, among other things, OCD and autism

underfull: in poker, a full house hand, where the pair is of a higher card rank than the set of three

witch's finger: a swollen, poisoned finger

NOTES

Stockholm Syndrome (16)
vertraue mir is German for 'trust me' (the reference is to the song 'Rose' by Bark Psychosis which uses it repeatedly).

Self, Rising (17)
Robert Wadlow is one of the tallest people who ever lived. There is a model of him outside the Ripley's Believe It or Not museum in central London.

Firebirds (20)
part of the legend of the phoenix is that only one can exist at any one time.

Women in Paintings (21)
Jill is Jill Hepple, a former student of mine who was often painted by her late husband, the portrait artist Norman Hepple.

Epithalamion (23)
this poem was written to be read at the wedding celebration of Sarah Howe and Marc Lixenberg.

Shanties of Tinie Hope (28)
Nemarca is the first name of a woman who wrote to the US band The Shins and asked if her unusual name could be included in a lyric. It appears in the song 'Phantom Limb': 'we're off to Nemarca's porch again.' *Crook Frightfulness* is the title of a book published in the 1930s by an anonymous writer who was cataloguing his paranoia – it remains a mysterious and cultish book.

Paul Risi (34)
Paul Risi was a Scottish songwriter and musician who died young in 1999.

A Small Photograph of the World Changing (40)
the quotes are from poems by Sarah Gridley and Brenda Shaugh-
nessy.

Bella (41)
Lord Shield Jaguar and Lady Xoc are Mayan figures who feature
on a stone lintel at The British Museum.

Halfway Through the Year of the Rabbit (68)
this poem was triggered by an occasion when I thought I was list-
ening to minimalist music, clicked to find the track name and found
that I was actually listening to silence. The Year of the Rabbit is
erroneous as there were no rabbits in China until recent centuries
– it should be Year of the Hare.

Jambhala's Mongoose (76)
Jambhala is a deity who is often depicted with a mongoose who
spits jewels. The unusual words in the poem are alternate words for
the symbol known as the swastika, with which he is also associated.

Fantigue (78)
in the early nineteenth century, there was a fad for hearing/fearing
'whistling ghosts' which is what Scott is referring to in the epigraph.

Solutomaattimittaamotulos (79)
From Finnish, and thought to be the world's longest single word
palindrome, its unlikely meaning is 'the result of a measurement in
a tomato laboratory'.

The Bells of Hope (95)
The Bells of Hope is a series of 51 poems, all of them in a short
form I developed, the kernel poem, in which truth (the 'kernel')
and metaphor swirl in one dimeter line and three equal, much
longer lines. These poems chart a time of change in my life, a year
when, for the only time in my life, I found myself living alone.
Originally intended to be a series of unconnected poems in this

form, inevitably, it became more of a diaristic sequence, recording situations, wishes and memories from one year.

'The Machine' (101): 'uniquely broken' was a phrase used by the hangman Albert Pierrepoint for the body of a hanged prisoner.

'The Ximenean' (106): in this sense refers not to the Inquisitor Ximenes, but to the crossword pioneer Derrick Macnutt who took his setter name from him. In the puzzle world, Ximenean refers to what is fair when constructing a crossword or other puzzle.

Roddy Lumsden's first book *Yeah Yeah Yeah* (1997) was shortlisted for Forward and Saltire prizes. His second collection *The Book of Love* (2000), a Poetry Book Society Choice, was shortlisted for the T.S. Eliot Prize. *Mischief Night: New & Selected Poems* (2004), a Poetry Book Society Recommendation, was followed by *Third Wish Wasted* (2009) and *Not All Honey* (2014), all these titles published by Bloodaxe Books, as was his anthology *Identity Parade: New British and Irish Poets* (2010).

He is a freelance writer, specialising in quizzes and word puzzles, and has held several residencies, including ones with the City of Aberdeen, St Andrews Bay Hotel, and as "poet-in-residence" to the music industry when he co-wrote *The Message*, a book on poetry and pop music (Poetry Society, 1999). His other books include *Vitamin Q: a temple of trivia, lists and curious words* (Chambers Harrap, 2004). Born in St Andrews, he lived in Edinburgh before moving to London.